HAUS CURIOSITIES

Art, Imagination and Public Service

About the Contributors

David Blunkett is a former Education and Employment Secretary and Home Secretary in Tony Blair's cabinet. He was an MP from 1987 until 2015, when he entered the House of Lords. He is currently Professor of Politics in Practice at the University of Sheffield. He is married with four sons and his home remains in Sheffield, where he was formerly leader of the council.

Micheal O'Siadhail is a poet. His *Collected Poems* was published in 2013, *One Crimson Thread* in 2015, and *The Five Quintets* in 2018. He was awarded an Irish American Cultural Institute prize for poetry (1982) and the Marten Toonder Award for Literature (1998). *The Five Quintets* was named the Conference on Christianity and Literature Book of the Year (2018) and received an Eric Hoffer Award (2020). He lives in New York.

Brenda Hale retired as President of the Supreme Court of the UK in January 2020, after twenty-six years as a full-time Judge in the High Court, Court of Appeal, House of Lords, and Supreme Court. Before that, she was an academic at Manchester University and then a Law Commissioner, specialising in family, welfare, and equality law.

Hughie O'Donoghue is a painter born in Manchester, with an MA in Fine Arts from Goldsmiths College, London. He was elected a Royal Academician in 2009. His major public commissions include stained glass windows for The Lady Chapel in Westminster Abbey and a painting, *St Martin Divides his Cloak*, for the Imperial Society of Knights Bachelor chapel in St Paul's Cathedral. He has been the subject of solo exhibitions at venues including Haus der Kunst in Munich, the Imperial War Museum in London, and the Irish Museum of Modern Art in Dublin.

Clare Moriarty was a civil servant for nearly thirty-five years, latterly as Permanent Secretary of the Department for Environment, Food & Rural Affairs and of the Department for Exiting the EU. She promotes people-centred leadership with an emphasis on diversity and inclusion, and speaks regularly about the importance of valuing emotion and creating space for difference. She is a lifelong choral singer and lover of nature.

James O'Donnell was appointed Organist and Master of the Choristers at Westminster Abbey in 2000. He read for a degree in Music at Jesus College, Cambridge, where he was an organ scholar and is now an Honorary Fellow. He was Master of Music at Westminster Cathedral from 1988 to 1999, and has also served as an Organ professor at the Royal Academy of Music and President of the Royal College of Organists.

Edited and with an introduction by
Claire Foster-Gilbert

ART, IMAGINATION AND PUBLIC SERVICE

David Blunkett, Micheal O'Siadhail
Brenda Hale, Hughie O'Donoghue
Clare Moriarty, James O'Donnell

First published by Haus Publishing in 2021
4 Cinnamon Row
London SW11 3TW
www.hauspublishing.com

A CIP catalogue record for this book is
available from the British Library

Print ISBN: 978-1-913368-18-0
Ebook ISBN: 978-1-913368-19-7

Typeset in Garamond by MacGuru Ltd

Printed in Czech Republic

Contents

Acknowledgements

Sincere thanks are due to the Dean and Chapter of Westminster, the Steering Group and Council of Reference of Westminster Abbey Institute, Asha Astley, Margaret Blunkett, Edoardo Braschi, Harry Hall, Alice Horne, Aneta Horniak, Kathleen James, Sam Laughton and the Elysian Singers, Seán Moore, Clare O'Donoghue, Barbara Schwepcke and Jo Stimfield.

Introduction

Claire Foster-Gilbert

If a politician or a judge or a civil servant takes time to look at a painting, or listen to music, or learn and recite a poem, will it make a positive difference to their public service? Monica Furlong writes:

> It can feel an eccentricity to settle one's tired body and mind down to pay attention to Shakespeare or Beethoven or an exhibition or an opera. But those who are addicts of such experiences know, as by a kind of faith, what they are about. However wearily and unwillingly they go they find themselves caught up, transformed by something outside themselves, which, without taking account of their particular problems, yet speaks to their universal condition.*

Art feeds the imagination and nourishes our souls. It

---

* Monica Furlong, *Contemplating Now* (London, 1971), 102.

helps us stay open and attuned to the deeper flows of life. Inevitably it will influence our beliefs, perceptions, and feelings, even though it can be hard to see exactly how.

Beliefs, perceptions, and feelings matter because they determine the way we see the world and how we respond to it. They work at the level of the disposition of a person rather than what he or she objectively chooses to attend to. They form our character and seep into our outward decisions and actions, even as we seek to apply reason and rationality to all we do. They are, then, subtle policy drivers.

Westminster Abbey Institute seeks to nourish the roots of public service, believing that our public servants, and the institutions through which they serve, do not think and decide and act from nowhere. The dispositions of people and institutions need conscious formation because humans are not well disposed (or for that matter ill disposed) by default. If attention is not paid to what underlies public service, then the public service itself can be corroded.

Here in our dispositions lurk the unconscious biases that unintentionally make some people outsiders as we fail to notice the ways in which we recognise and promote those whom we feel are like ourselves. Here is the place where the charismatic politician is in danger of believing their own emotive rhetoric, employed to garner support, amounting to no more than empty populism. And here is where, even as science's contribution to public policy is being outwardly recognised and championed, we are confounded by conspiracy theories whose influence is visceral, impossible to counter with rational argument.

Rational argument, rigorous gathering of evidence, impartial representation, and equitable distribution of services are vital to public service. All these provisions are meted out by human beings, though, with inevitably partial perception, an inadequate grasp of all the facts, and numerous unconscious biases. Artificial or enhanced intelligence can help. But computer systems themselves have baked-in biases from the unconscious priorities of programmers.

One might think that the solution to excellent public service is to create full perception; enable the grasping of all relevant facts; remove the unconscious biases; forbid charismatic people from standing for political office. But were we to achieve such a godlike – or rather a quantum computer-like – state, we would, I suggest, have also removed our humanity, which is essential to great public service and leadership. The non-utilitarian, incommensurable, numerically indefinable place where beliefs and perceptions sit is a dangerous place, but we need it. Belief in conspiracy theories is irrational, but openness to the as-yet-unknown is not. Empty populist rhetoric misdirects loyalty, but good rhetoric induces powerful, courage-building emotions of loyalty and love. Distorted love unconsciously discriminates against the other, but protective love and service can be available to all. And it is in the very recognition of our propensity to see only partially and to believe mistakenly that humility is engendered. Hard on humility's heels comes the willingness to learn from those mistakes. It is our humility that enables us to continue to learn and grow and understand further and keep asking questions – in short, to evolve.

The feelings and perceptions that form our dispositions have, then, to be attended to; fed with good company; oriented towards the good; made resilient to the corrosive temptations of power. Art creates a pathway to feelings and perceptions, but how does it then affect our dispositions? Will it nourish them in such a way that public service is strengthened? And can it do more than that? Can it speak into the process of political leadership, justice, and policymaking as well as feeding the dispositions of those who enact these public service roles? Can it – should it – influence institutions as well as people?

Art might be nothing more than a distraction. Or it could ask disconcerting questions, undermining tried-and-tested ways of working but replacing them with nothing constructive. It might dissipate our public servants' focus on getting the job done – and on ensuring they have the necessary numerical skills, big data literacy, and computational ability. Or it might ensure that public service is not just utilitarian. It might work on the disposition of a public servant so that they are able to free themself from tightly held beliefs. It might help with creating the visionary imagination to address the seemingly intractable problems of the twenty-first century, such as the apparently incompatible demands of feeding the world and cooling the planet, or keeping everyone safe and also free.

In order to find out if art helps public service, Westminster Abbey Institute constructed three dialogues between practitioners: a politician and a poet; a judge and a painter; a civil servant and a musician. The dialogue partners were willing to explore the question, but it wasn't easy. The conversations demanded an openness to seemingly very different worlds. Our three public servants are constrained by, respectively, public opinion; the system of the courts; and careful and comprehensive analysis of evidence. Our artists, by the nature of their task, have to be free to burst beyond the bounds of what is known and understood, and pursue through imagination and vision what most of us cannot yet see and certainly cannot measure. Often, as the artist Hughie O'Donoghue says, they do not know what they are doing, and the dialogues required them to try to articulate something that felt beyond words. But the conversations produced some surprising commonalities as well as a great deal of sympathy. In each case, the public servant could see the value of the arts even though that value was, by its very nature, not utilitarian, commensurable, or formally useful. The discoveries and observations were of lasting interest, and so edited versions of the conversations are offered here.

Micheal O'Siadhail, the poet in dialogue with the politician David Blunkett, has a facility with words and, as it turns out, a great deal of valuable insight into public service, as the dialogue shows. Political leaders share with poets the challenge of adding their bit: their words, their style of leadership, their idea or policy they believe will help make the world a better place, when the greatest minds have bent to this task over and over again before them. So also a poet might think: how can I dare to add my words to those of the great poets of yesteryear? And yet they must, understanding that their contribution is not likely to be world shattering but incremental, and being content with that.

Poets and politicians also share the challenge of trying to find a vehicle, a form to convey their ideas. It is not enough to have a strong feeling of beauty or justice: one must work to bring it to birth in the world. Poetry has the form provided by metre, the sound of words, the length of lines, the shape of a stanza, at which the poet has to work hard in order to speak their truth. Politicians need formal policies and slow-growing, sustainable institutions to ensure their ideas are carried through into law and practice.

No less importantly, Blunkett mourns his disconnection with art when, he now believes, he needed it most: in the thick of his political career. He wishes that he had had ways of ensuring that he still heard birdsong, took time to listen to his heart, while he was constantly assailed by the challenges of his work not just as a cabinet minister but also as he was seeking election and re-election: the ceaseless call to retain power. He acknowledges that by failing to connect to art, because it did not serve his immediate purposes and he had no spare time at all for it, he was in some vital way disconnecting from his own humanity, and he needed his humanity in order to be a good politician, a good servant of the electorate. It looks like a paradox: that which serves his humanity appears to be a distraction. Westminster Abbey Institute has seen that this is the greatest challenge for MPs: to make time to feed their own souls even as they are seeking to retain their democratic power and adequately serve those they represent. It feels hard to justify, selfish even, but the work on disposition is not a distraction, it is an essential part of what it takes to be a politician.

In the dialogue between the visual artist Hughie O'Donoghue and the judge Brenda Hale, we learn from both how 'truth is a fugitive thing' (O'Donoghue). What makes an artist's work compelling is its commitment to telling the truth, which can never be finally achieved; the work is alive with the active attempt. O'Donoghue suggests Vincent van Gogh is the greatest artist of all time for this reason: not because his paintings are very good, he says, but because Van Gogh never lost that commitment, costly though it was to him personally. The more surprising element of the dialogue, though, is the admission by Hale of the elusiveness of truth in her world. It has to be discovered, over and over again: a fugitive thing. Of course, she allows, there is a kind of stable truth: the speed limit is 30 mph, and if you go over it you will have committed a criminal offence. But principles in law which we might regard as universally true are not so: for example, the achievement of equality before the law is quite new. Now the law takes no account of irrelevant details such as a person's gender, sexuality, or ethnicity, but this understanding of social equality has only emerged in Hale's lifetime; it is an achievement of the law of which she is most proud. It is very, very recent.

What other undiscovered biases are written into the judicial system because they sit unquestioned in our own dispositions? We can never imagine we have come to the end of the truth and found its final expression. Artists teach us that. So, again, they also teach humility.

The third dialogue, between the civil servant Clare Moriarty and the musician James O'Donnell, is produced here as a reflection written by Moriarty, arising from their conversation rather than in dialogue form. Moriarty writes of the connection and creativity – the beauty – that is to be found in making, performing, and listening to music, and of her wish, longing even, to find that in the heart of her policymaking. If connection with people is not included in policymaking from the start, policies can be technically perfect, theoretically neat and tidy, perfectly formed, but nearly useless once implementation takes place and they meet the unpredictable complexity of human lives. But such inclusion of the mess of humanity in policymaking militates against tidy formulae. The value and purpose of policymaking lie deeper than the technicalities: they are to be found in the creative imagination, which is open to the new in a different way from a computer-like approach, which just seeks to broaden its bandwidth to assimilate more and more data. The process is mysterious, or rather it feels mysterious until one looks back and sees that one did in fact know something, one just didn't know what it was exactly, and it presented itself first as a feeling. Moriarty writes of her growing trust in her intuitions as they increasingly stood up to rational scrutiny. She also writes of her growing awareness of the centrality of people in policymaking, both in creating and leading teams and in folding the public into the process – not just the implementation – of policy. Such an approach is what true leadership is made of, and it includes the need to attend to one's own self-development in the role, because the role is fulfilled as much by who you are as by what you do. Musicians recognise this: they will typically spend 95 per cent of their time practising and only 5 per cent – and not even that during the pandemic – performing. Musicians also recognise the centrality of people: those by whom music is performed and those for whom it is performed. Other people make music, like policy, messier but truer, closer to what it is trying to say or be. Moreover, the audience gives the performers energy. The audience is their life-blood, the air they breathe. Likewise: what is a public servant without a public to serve? The artists in our dialogues teach us that humility.

If the dialogues worked, they did so because the dialogue partners were up for the challenge. The public servants were prepared to enter and explore the dangerous territory where disposition is formed, where beliefs and feelings and perceptions lurk. The artists, for whom this territory is familiar, were prepared to be guides, and in so doing to take the risk of trying to articulate tender truths that do not easily enter the light of discourse because they know they are threatened by scorn, lack of understanding, impatience, and the dreadful measurements that utility demands. The dialogues and essay make evident the wisdom of the three public servants and the insight of the artists. They evoke delight, flair, new ideas, and a greater responsiveness and sensitivity to public service. They demonstrate what Furlong's addicts somehow know but have constantly to relearn.

Ruling from the Heart:
The Poet and the Cabinet Minister

*A dialogue between David Blunkett
and Micheal O'Siadhail*

Introduction by David Blunkett

This dialogue is an edited version of a conversation that took place in Westminster Abbey in November 2019 between Micheal O'Siadhail, a poet, and myself, a politician and former cabinet minister. The dialogue explores how poetry can enable politics to connect with the heart, not just the head. Our conversation took place in the middle of a general election, and I was very aware at the time of the lack, in our public dialogues, of this connection between politics and the poetic and spiritual. I feel very strongly how important it is that people feel in their hearts as well as in their heads what it is that they expect and want from political dialogue and the political arena. The perspective of the poet then was timely. It will always be timely.

*

Micheal O'Siadhail

Westminster Abbey Institute concerns itself with matters of moral and spiritual courage, and with the compass of public service, in the case of both individuals and institutions. We are here in Parliament Square, with the Palace of Westminster, Whitehall, the Supreme Court, and, of course, this Abbey on each of the four sides. With so many public servants about their business here, the air must constantly rain with 'yes, minister', or even 'yes, prime minister'. This puts me in mind of a very early lyric poem of mine called 'Spring', which I published in my first ever collection of poems. I'd like to read it as a prologue to our dialogue because it says 'yes, minister' to the ultimate Minister:

I saw one morning at nine,
A bird on the run for all its worth
From tree No. 1,
A public servant moving heaven and earth,
To see his master's will is done,
In tree No. 2,

And almost unbeknownst to me
If I hadn't heard on the grapevine,
That he'd a wire from his minister
To tell how another year

Returns. Nothing amiss.
Just as everything should be, it is.

I'm very aware of how much experience David has of being in government, with all its pressures and responsibilities. I, for my part, work at a far more contemplative level. However, I'm not a complete innocent; I have, in my time, had a taste of politics in both academia and the arts. Harold Wilson, the former leader of your party, David, once remarked that he left academia and went into national politics because academic politics were far too dirty.

In my work, I range from the intensely personal to exploring public themes such as the Holocaust, globalisation, and language. My latest book, *The Five Quintets*, is most relevant to this dialogue. I spent ten years writing *The Five Quintets*, which is a Dante-like meditation on modernity through imagined conversations with the movers and shakers of the last 400 years or so. There's a quintet on each of the arts, as well as economics, politics, science, and philosophy and theology. Those involved in public service will know how all these themes interweave to create the polyphony we call society. For the purposes of this dialogue, however, I would like to separate out each theme in order to find clues as to how we might best rule from the heart.

First, the arts. Contemplating artists of the past 400 years, I am convinced that the greatest of them keep both heart and mind in tandem, hold both emotion and intellect in tension. George Herbert knew the world of ruling, and was one of the finest poets ever, in my view, in the English language. In *The Five Quintets*, I have him say:

I know my worth; I know power's thrill and sheen;
For me sour grapes don't hang too high above,
I know too well what mirth and music mean,
I know the ways of learning yet I love.

For rulers and administrators, the temptation must surely be to take too rigid a stance – to be too unbending, to be Creon, refusing burial, rather than Antigone, yielding to her compassion. For the sake of neatness, for the sake of absolute consistency, it must be so easy to forget we rule not for the sake of ruling but, rather, to further human flourishing. Literature, painting, sculpture, and music must allow us to rule from the heart, to remain in touch with our own feelings, to ensure we don't lose compassion, joy, and abandon. As I ask the ultimate Minister in the epigraph to *The Five Quintets*:

In words and hues and tones, please, Madam, blow,

Play in me the grace I need to know,
How in your complex glory we let go.

Second, economics. What can economics say to the
question of ruling from the heart? Clearly good man-
agement of resources is part of it. But as I looked at the
major figures in economics across modernity, it became
gradually clear to me that neither totalitarian ideologues
nor free marketeers rule from the heart. I believe that
the best economists, such as John Maynard Keynes and
Amartya Sen, have understood that ruling from the heart
involves both justice and generosity. The head demands
justice; the heart demands generosity. In my ventrilo-
quism in *The Five Quintets*, I make Keynes say:

I've been a civil servant and I know
So much is chance and how most change is slow;
I peak between the crash of '29
And World War Two and, forced to switch my tack,
I think beyond the ledger's bottom line.

Or, to return to my epigraph, where I address the ultimate Minister:

Show how an open hand is worry-free,
Spark again your love's economy,

Your generous first words spoken 'Let there be'.

The third quintet in this societal polyphony deals with politics, and clearly this is central to ruling from the heart. There's no doubt that we have to steer the ship of state. We have to rule. Yet reviewing the 400 years or so of modernity, the curse has always been extreme ideologues, both left and right. Extreme ideologues have been ready to sacrifice all on their altars in the hope of starting with some *tabula rasa*, believing that we can wipe the slate clean, that we can start from scratch. I'm convinced that to rule from the heart in politics means to keep seeking the best combination of realism and compassion. Realism without compassion risks simply becoming arid and inhuman. It can fall easily into hollow, utilitarian ways. But compassion without realism seems to me to be doomed to fail. For example, the Flower Power movement of the sixties went simply nowhere – it was followed by a swing to that great ambition of the 'go for it' generation.

Alongside this fusion of realism and compassion, I think we need the humility to know that all our best efforts fall short. I think of the Jewish concept of *Tikkun Olam*: the mending of the universe. There is no perfection. To rule from the heart, we have to be happy just to keep on trying to make the world a little less imperfect.

As I engaged with the lives of politicians throughout modernity, several stood out for me as having the moral and spiritual resources to change, to journey towards deeper understanding, to rule from the heart. Among those were William Gladstone, Mahatma Gandhi, and Nelson Mandela. I imagine Gladstone saying:

Dare I ask if you all journeyed too?
Speaking for myself I know I did.
Though prime minister you see I lead
First the Tories, then the Liberals—
After all I spanned a century.
Once high Tory under Robert Peel
I believed that church and state are one,
I become a Liberal who tries
Slowly to remove the barriers
Of both class and creed that still curbed growth.
Church of Ireland's disestablishment
I achieved, though many disapproved;
I introduced the secret ballot box.
So although Home Rule for Ireland failed
I prepared an empire's unseen end;
Even if I'm of my times I guide
People towards another century
Following the paths I pioneered.

And in the epigraph I write:

> Enhance our trust in hard-earned betterment,
> Humbler world we may in turn augment
> In long adagios of increment.

Fourth, let's consider science. The dream of the Enlightenment was a mechanical vision of complete mastery. Many of you will recall Karl Marx's famous dictum, that religion was the opium of the people, but one wag said, echoing Marx, 'Progress was the opium of the Enlightenment'. I think we have since learned that we're part of nature. Werner Heisenberg has shown that we can't observe without affecting what we observe. We have to learn a new humility. We can't tie down the subatomic dance. And more, we're still in a rapid technological revolution that has changed our ways of living fundamentally. What could such technology in a malign regime lead to? Are we in danger of becoming a shallow technocracy? Without a doubt, our damaged and threatened planet must now be our focus. If we're to survive, ruling from the heart in science means a fresh respect for creation, an old wonder, a new humility. From the epigraph:

> While marvelling at your choreography,

Stars and quarks beyond our mastery,
We still explore to praise your mystery.

The fifth and last quintet is about philosophy and theology. If we are to rule from the heart, we cannot ignore the thinkers who have asked the big questions about the meaning of our brief sojourn, who have tried to make sense of it all, who have grappled with the meaning of our tiny lives on this planet.

In this quintet I have traversed thought's trajectory across modernity, keeping the larger framework of our existence in mind. I've conversed with many theologians and philosophers. I've seen how our behaviour is coloured by how God is envisaged, and I've seen how we might rule in so many subtle and indirect ways. Martin Luther is one of the theologians with whom I have my imagined conversations, and I have him say:

In Psalms and Romans too again I find
Therein the righteousness of God revealed;
As sinners, pardon for our human kind

Depends on grace; who God decides is healed
And all our excursions wasted sweat.
By faith and faith alone our fates are sealed.

And I have Karl Barth, one of the greatest theologians of modernity, say:

> God is God above our human mind,
> beyond ourselves and still beyond beyond;
> and free as light that can delight or blind.

A third, Hans Urs von Balthasar who is sometimes called the Catholic Barth, says:

> As infants in our mother's smile we learn,
> for all the gap between our God and us,
> it is for love's analogy we yearn.

If it is really for love's analogy we yearn, we most certainly will side more with the compassionate Antigone than the harder-hearted Creon.

I have at this point just two tentative suggestions to offer of possible parallels, corresponding qualities, between the artistic process and ruling from the heart. The first might be courage. In the light of all the great poetry, or music, or painting that exists, how can anyone have the nerve to think that they can come up with something else? A new work that can stand comparison with previous masterpieces? How can I dare to think I can? And surely a politics that rules from the heart demands a similar audacity. To imagine, after thousands of years of human endeavour, that you can possibly propose a change that will make the world a fraction less imperfect. How can you dare to make what *is* a little bit better? But you must.

A second parallel might be the working out of inspiration. A poem may begin with a mix of a notion and a hum. How that moves along must remain open to the constraints of thought and shape, until, holding content and form in tension, it comes somehow to match up to the pressure of that original inspiration. And I can't help thinking that for politics ruling from the heart, an initiative begins with both an insight into where there's a need and some concept of betterment. Yet, similar to the artistic process, politicians must surely navigate between the realism of circumstance and the ideal to which they aspire, until it measures up, at least to some degree, to their initial insight. This final extract is from the quintet on politics and says what I mean here:

> Our ancients knew, whatever shapes the ship,
> A state is steered. This is a trope the Greeks
> Alcaeus and Aeschylus long ago
> And Plato in his dream *Republic* would
> Refine their metaphor to tell us how
> We sailors on such unknown seas that toss

And change must choose a helmsman for our ship.
For him, philosophers are best to helm.
...
The fantasists of left and right both fail
To see how states must ground stability,
How institutions take so long to grow;
Yet like a tree unleafed they too can wilt
And neither Marxists nor free-marketeers,
Despite their fantasies, can find a way
To keep what's brutish, nasty, brief at bay.
...
Perhaps we learn a little from the past.
Though paradigms of history repeat,
They also shift or slowly rearrange
The models we assume, so we can know
Something of what's best and so can build
From age to age as wisely as we may.
Let's try to trace our own trajectory
For though we can no longer now believe
In linear advance, we still may learn
From stories of adaption and mistakes,
Aware how we arrived at where we are.
Refining our inheritance, attuned
Anew to what is new, we dare to change.

Then where is poetry in politics?

So many counted syllables in all
The cut and thrust? No more and yet no less
Than lines in our polyphony of thought
That shapes an ambience in which we act.
Epiphanies occur, thoughts percolate
To shape adaptions we may learn to dare.
And no one knows how syllables are weighed.

We travel towards a star we're steering by
To one imagined harbour's havened dream.

David Blunkett

Thank you Micheal. You mentioned Flower Power. There have been many causes, the latest being Extinction Rebellion, whose promoters don't necessarily know how to, or even wish to, link to the formal political process. We've seen that over generations. One example, however, of where the just cause did lead to real change was Make Poverty History. In the period leading up to the G8 of 2005, there was a real upsurge particularly from young people with a passion and a desire, not a mechanistic view, but a real commitment to overcoming the inequality and injustice in the world. Some progress was made, because the massive cross-border campaign did actually lead, in July 2005, to commitments made in the G8 to debt redemption in sub-Saharan Africa and on climate change. And I just wanted to explore that with you. How can we link the passion that exists to the reality of decision-making?

Micheal O'Siadhail

I came to manhood in the sixties, when we all believed we had the answer to everything. We were going to change the world, and we knew exactly what was to be done. But it was a terrible naivety. Nothing changes just from passion. We didn't get into the institutions and change them from within. I don't know what the answer is, but I understand the question: how do we harness that extraordinary idealism of youth and passion to bring about changes through the institutions we have?

David Blunkett

As Education and Employment Secretary, as a Secretary of State, I had to follow the rules. I found it was much easier to be in the straitjacket of following rules, because the minute you step out of them you can be accused of all kinds of things that actually cause you great grief. There was an occasion when I was approached by some family members of a young woman who'd just taken her GCSEs and was waiting for the results, and they told me that her mother was dying, and it was quite likely, given the prognosis, that her mother would die before the August date when the GCSE results would be sent out. Would I, somehow, get the examining board to let the mother have the results, because everyone believed that this young woman was going to do really well? And I was advised, very strongly, not to. But I decided that there was no point in being the Secretary of State if you couldn't actually do things. So, I persuaded the examining board, under very strict conditions, to supply the results before they were announced. And I informed the family, who then told me that other family members thought this was an extremely bad idea, and that it was likely to disrupt the mother's final hours, and would I not do it? I tell this story because it is an example of how I'd put my neck on the block, only to find, in the end, it was chopped off. The difficulty with this sort of experience is that it makes you more immune to appeals to your heart. The tendency is to go back into your box and to accept advice when you're asked not to do things. It didn't do this to me completely, though. When I was Home Secretary, a trip to France had been arranged for a school in Rotherham. There was only one student in the class who was not going to be able to go on the school trip, because his father was an asylum seeker and he had no clearance of papers, and therefore the boy had no means of returning. The parent approached me and asked if there was anything I could do about it. I reminisced a bit in my head about the previous occasion, and talked to the very good civil servants in my private office, and we decided that we'd find a way of doing it. And the boy did go, and he did come back, and his father was eternally grateful. So, there are times when you can break the mould, and you get some satisfaction back, but all of us are human, so, if there'd been a second occasion when things had gone badly wrong, I suspect I would have gone back in the box and never come out again.

Micheal O'Siadhail

It reminds me that 'hard cases make bad law'. It is really a question of discernment, but I'm sure that, if you go on the side of the angels and get yourself into trouble a couple of times, you can become immune to the pleas.

David Blunkett

It is even harder not to become immune to your own humanity when you are in the thick of the most difficult issues. I was made Home Secretary by Tony Blair in June 2001. I'd only been Home Secretary for three weeks when the Parole Board decided to release the two young men who had murdered the infant James Bulger. You can imagine the *Daily Mail*, *Express*, and, well, most of the media actually, were on my back. It was rapidly followed by the 11 September attacks in New York and

Pennsylvania. I found myself not overwhelmed, but shut out from the things that had been really important to me in private: to read poetry, to listen to music, to understand the connection with nature, and birdsong. And I found it really hard to hang on to those normal human traits that leaven us and make it possible for us to be rounded. And I still, today, look back and think, was there more I could have done to cling on to those really critical elements that kept me human?

In the election of 1992, when I'd been in Parliament for five years, I was a frontbencher expecting to be a minister in the Kinnock government. We expected to be elected, but we lost. I came back from the count in my own constituency, where of course I'd been re-elected, and I went outside. It was dawn, and I heard a blackbird. What struck me was that the world was still going on, that, for most people, nothing had changed, that the world revolved, the sun shone, and nature continued to struggle to survive.

So, I want to explore this question with you: through poetry and music, and with that link to the natural environment around us, could we reach people in a way that we don't often think about? I doubt if the party manifestos for this coming election will make more than a nodding, passing reference to culture of any kind. Wouldn't it be wonderful if, as well as providing free broadband, we were promising that we would elevate poetry and the understanding of well-being in our schools?

Micheal O'Siadhail

Yes. My roots of poetry are in the schoolbooks. I still remember the poems that I learned when I was eight, nine, ten, and I just thought it was pure magic, and the rest of my life has been shaped by that, and if you're not exposed to that possibility in schools, if you're not given the excitement of poetry then, I am not sure you can find it later.

David Blunkett

I want to read you a poem I wrote a long time ago. If someone hadn't said this was a poem, I wouldn't have necessarily known it was one. I wrote it when I went to Wimbledon to see the tennis tournament, thirty years ago, when Chris Evert and Steffi Graf were in the women's semi-final, and it goes something like this:

Centre Court cocooned,
Warm and comfortable, untouched by accents alien
   to our own.
People who think they own all about them,
Enjoying the sunshine, melting in the heat.

Togetherness born of easy friendship and shared
   experience.

(You can see this is a political poem.)

The ancient grounds green and spacious,
The scent of strawberries and hay.
Grass roasting in the midday sun.
Centre Court, tension,
Click of ball on racket,
The echo. The call of umpire,
Quiet please, we're thinking.

I was trying to express two things in that poem: firstly,
yes, the accents were all very much the same; the homo-
geneity has broken down a bit over the last thirty years
but, to get to Centre Court for the semi-final, you had
to know somebody; and, secondly, there was no internet
then or social media, but I was very aware of 'the echo',
because now we have, so often, an echo of our own thinking, and people echo each other's thoughts on social
media. So, Micheal, is it a poem or merely an expression,
a stream of consciousness?

Micheal O'Siadhail
The thing to remember, always, is that poetry is art. If

it were simply emotion, or a deep feeling about something, you could go up to the top of a hill and let it all out, whereas in art, you're crafting something, and you're using the tradition of that art to craft it in such a way that you marry content and form. When you get the content and the form to marry beautifully, you've made a beautiful poem. The definitions, of course, are endless. One friend of mine, when he was asked what poetry was, would answer, 'It's the stuff that doesn't go to the edges.' I think it's intensified emotion that's crafted in a way that catches the pulse of what you're trying to say, and communicates that emotion and thought to another.

Audience member

Would you agree that, if you don't know whether it's poetry, it isn't?

Micheal O'Siadhail

The ultimate question for me, in all forms of art, is: does it move me, does it leave me feeling I'm a richer human being at the end of it?

I love form, because it shapes poetry. In *The Five Quintets* I use 'saikus' (a mixture of sonnets and haikus, with the meaning in Japanese of 'a fine piece of work'), *terza rima* (triplets), and iambic pentameter, and I invent forms. I like the classical and the invented. The content is influenced by the form, and the form influences the content; there's a dynamic going on the whole time with it. It is a marriage.

I wouldn't, at the same time, dismiss all free verse. The wonderful thing about free verse is that it broke the sing-song effect of traditional poetry, so now when you actually rhyme, you do it voluntarily. It's not compulsory, as it once was. But, as I say, my ultimate test for all art, but particularly for poetry, is: does it move me? Does it move my heart and my mind, and does it leave me feeling a little more compassionate, a little more enriched?

Audience member
Lord Blunkett, you presided over quite an interesting time in the aftermath of 9/11, as you mentioned, but also race riots in Bradford, and Oldham, and Burnley. Those events began some conversations about integration in the UK, and I'm curious about what role you think art and culture have to play in producing that national unity?

David Blunkett
I inherited those riots. They'd started during the general election, which is highly unusual, and continued immediately afterwards. Communities had been whipped up into antagonism and division by other people who walked away. That has been a historic fact of life,

where people cause division but don't have to face its consequences.

I have found that the best ways of getting people to work together, to understand together, to learn about each other's history and background, and their humanity, have been through music, dance, art, and occasionally – but not often enough – through poetry. Barriers broke down when people, particularly young people, came together through art. The dance at festivals, the music, got people to understand and appreciate each other and themselves.

Art has a massive part to play in healing those wounds of division, but also in getting people to understand that they are just the same human beings, and that their background can be shared and enjoyed together.

Micheal O'Siadhail

I think that works also, David, on a personal basis. I mean, the thing that struck me as a boy, with poetry, was to suddenly realise that the deep feelings I had were shared by somebody else. When you read a Shakespeare sonnet about love, when you yourself have fallen in love, you realise this has been going on for 500 years. To know you're not alone is an extraordinary effect of art. Without art, how would you know? This, I think, is our common humanity, that very few people go through teenage years without attempting, in the flux of feeling, to write a love poem, or to write a lament for a parent, or some other emotional event. Some of us never get over this impulse, and continue to attempt to express our thoughts and feelings, but for all of us I think poetry is how you know that you're human, you know that others live with thoughts and feelings resembling your own.

David Blunkett
The same goes for people who have had the experience of escape from danger, from conflict, or from just unacceptable conditions. R. S. Thomas wrote a poem called 'The Evacuee'. The first line is:

> She woke up under a loose quilt
> Of leaf patterns, woven by the light

Art makes it possible for people to express their own feelings, their own tragedy, as well as their joy. I've often wondered why it is that so much glorious art comes from hurt as well as from love.

Audience member
This is a question for you both. Micheal, you introduced us to the winning world of the head demanding justice, and the heart demanding generosity. I also wonder if it

can work the other way around: the heart can demand justice from a virtue perspective, and the head can demand generosity. And I wonder if that opens up two other potentials of contact between the world of politics and the arts, because if the head is demanding generosity, it opens the space for the imagination to work, and for binaries to break down in an interesting way. Would you both offer your thoughts?

David Blunkett
It opens the way to breaking the mould, but in politics, that is both a plus and a minus. I'm a radical and some-times, painfully, I've had to dissociate myself from what I've wanted to do. For example, I found it really hard to try to keep the balance between having strong and understandable border controls, and having compas-sion for people's needs as refugees. I felt the need of the individuals who wrote or came to my advice surgery. It was very hard to confine myself within the public policy envelope when I knew that if I broke out of it, I would be actually making policy that would then push boundaries beyond anything that had been agreed with colleagues. I found that really hard.

Micheal O'Siadhail
You're obviously talking from experience, whereas I'm

more at a theoretical level. But if art does anything, it breaks down that binary between the heart and the mind; it brings both together. So, I have no trouble at all in saying the head is demanding compassion and the heart is demanding justice. Amartya Sen's book *The Idea of Justice* recognises this.

May I ask you, David, which politicians in the past and even, dare to say, in the present, you find inspirational?

David Blunkett

Without equivocation, I regard Nelson Mandela as inspirational. It was a privilege to have met him. I found Bill Clinton quite inspiring because of his personality. There's no question that, when he walked into a room, you knew he was there, with all his faults as well as his charisma. I would also speak of the leader of the Council I joined as a very young and immature new councillor. No one will have heard of him. He was a really inspirational guy because he encouraged without patronising. It's very easy, when you have some form of disability, to find that people patronise you, and they don't tell you the truth.

Sometimes the inspirational person is outside the political arena. It's the mum who comes to your advice surgery, and she's got three or four children under ten, and she's living in a high-rise, and she's struggling with two jobs to make ends meet, and all she wants is to get some tax credit problem sorted out that's been going on for months. That is a person of inspiration, in my view.

Audience member

Is it true that we're losing the power of oratory, or are we just not listening to the form that it's taking now? My teenage daughter is trying to persuade me of the value of rap, and I'm thinking about the enormous influence that some rap artists have currently, particularly amongst young people. Would you consider rap a form of poetry?

Micheal O'Siadhail

I have mixed feelings about rap. I had two teenage step-sons, one of whom played a great deal of rap, and I'm afraid the only words I was able to make out were usually expletives. I also work looking out on the East River in New York, and underneath my window runs the FDR freeway from where it seems cars keep blaring rap from their radios. So, I have ambiguous feelings towards it. But I come back to my question: does it actually move these kids? Does it make them feel that the world is richer? Does it give them compassion? I can't answer because I haven't heard enough of it or understood enough of it to know. I really can't tell.

David Blunkett

Could I ask if your daughter has been listening to George the Poet? He's a rapper.

Audience member

I'm afraid I don't know. She's trying to educate me but failing miserably.

David Blunkett

I just wanted you to say how impressed you were that I'd heard of him.

Audience member

Lord Blunkett, now, in this country, what needs to be done to defend politics?

David Blunkett

First: rebuild a degree of trust. There'll not always be trust in politics and politicians, because we fail as human beings. But we can rebuild a degree of trust by much greater honesty about what the struggle is and how difficult it is, rather than giving people to believe that we can wave a magic wand and make everything all right, which only leads to disillusionment. Secondly, therefore, try to be an educator, to explain where the sources of power lie, and what we need to do about power. And thirdly, and crucially, engage with active citizenship. If politics is about what's happening in this square, Parliament Square, then we're doomed, because people will see it as something that is done unto them, and they expect people to do it for them, rather than engaging with it in a way that actually makes it possible for us to do it together, so that people feel they're engaged in that political struggle as well.

Audience member

Could I play devil's advocate for a minute? When we look at the news here every day, we see a lot of inflamed passions. Are we perhaps being ruled too much from the heart and too little by the head?

David Blunkett

I think that manipulation of the political dialogue has been honed over recent years. The use of clever psychology, not to touch people's hearts but to inflame their feelings, goes back centuries, and it is being deployed now. Unless we understand the interplay of that psychology with the political process in the political arena, we will be manipulated again. Goebbels manipulated the people through film, the Soviet Union through art, and we see it today in Trump and Putin as they turn people against people. It is happening in this country too. If we understand it, then we can countervail it by sensible, honest argument, but also by means of emotion and passion, to turn people against hate and prejudice.

We need our poets. Over the generations, dictators and demagogues have not been able to ban poetry, which can speak that which would otherwise have put people in prison. Poetry can speak a message that can be conveyed in ways that tyrants have not been able to set aside.

Micheal O'Siadhail

The dichotomy of heart and mind is false; the question is how we bring both together. It is the ultimate art, to do this. The art of politics is to bring the energetic passion of the young together with the form which is found in our institutions. Both in art and in politics the question is: how do you get the feeling and the form together? How can we have young people realise that their passion has to be channelled through institutions which actually change society, rather than just letting it all float in the air? The question is parallelled in the difference between good and bad poetry. We all, as teenagers, have let out the passion in words, but the shaping of the passion, the sweat it takes to shape a poem, to shape a piece of music, to shape anything of art into something that moves you, both through its form and through its content, is I think the same. Achieving such a fusion is the challenge for both politicians and poets.

Envisioning Justice:
The Painter and the Judge

A dialogue between Brenda Hale and
Hughie O'Donoghue

Introduction by Brenda Hale

This dialogue is an edited version of a conversation between the artist Hughie O'Donoghue and me in Westminster Abbey in November 2019. It took place shortly after the Supreme Court, of which I was President at the time, had ruled that the government had acted unlawfully in advising The Queen to prorogue Parliament. There was a lot of comment and criticism about that judgment and the role of judges in general, so it was a timely opportunity to say something about how the Justices of the Supreme Court produce judgments. But the dialogue was about much more than that: Hughie O'Donoghue and I were able to explore how his endeavours as an artist compare and contrast with those of a judge in the search for truth.

*

Brenda Hale

I have brought with me a prop, the personification of Justice, as she is normally depicted. She is a blindfolded woman holding scales and a sword. The scales are a very early image associated with judging and justice, dating back as far as Babylonian times, denoting balance or fairness. The sword could go back to Old Testament times, and the story of the judgement of Solomon: he proposed to cut a baby in half with his sword, since two women were claiming to be its mother. His judgment revealed the real mother, because she immediately dropped her claim rather than see her child cut in half. That story gave rise to the saying 'the wisdom of Solomon', and may be the origin of Justice wielding a sword. There is also the story of St Michael, who appears in the Old Testament as an advocate for the Jews and in the New Testament as a sword-wielding defeater of Satan. The sword indicates that judges are both to judge and to punish. The blindfold has a more equivocal origin. Early images showed Justice without a blindfold. It came to be associated, later on, with impartiality, and that is how we can understand it today. But its origin may be in a woodcut attributed to Dürer, published in Sebastian Brant's *Ship of Fools* in 1494, entitled 'The Fool Blindfolding Justice', denoting stupidity or failure to see what is in front of one.

So, with Justice duly looking over us, as she did in the

original dialogue, I would like to say something about how judges work before we hear how artists work from Hughie.

Judges seek to be influenced by the evidence when they are determining facts, and by the legal materials and reasoning when they are determining the legal principles applicable to those facts. The Supreme Court, the highest court in the land and the place of final appeal, only determines legal principles. It is not a trial court, so it doesn't decide facts; the lower courts do that. The cases that come to us in the Supreme Court raise arguable points of law of general public importance.

A typical Supreme Court judgment goes like this: firstly, we try to encapsulate the issue in the first paragraph or two, articulating what the case is about and what the legal problem is. Secondly, we set out the relevant facts, and how the case has been decided in the lower courts – typically the original trial court and the Court of Appeal. Thirdly, we try to explain the relevant legal materials, that is, the legislation and previously decided cases. Unlike the lower courts, the Supreme Court is not bound to follow cases decided in other courts, which gives us much more freedom than they have. We can even, if necessary in the interests of justice, depart from previous decisions at Supreme Court level. So, we don't have to spend a long time trying to reconcile and deduce principles from the lower court decisions. We are always guided by the underlying principles of law but, by definition, we are deciding something to which the answer is not clear, so we are to some extent making new law in every case. Fourthly, we explain what the arguments are on either side of the issue and, fifthly, we explain how we reach our own conclusion.

We sit in panels of five, seven, nine, or – on two occasions in my time – all eleven of us. We try to have a single lead judgment representing the decision and the reasoning of the majority. From this, it becomes clear what the *ratio decidendi* of the case is. The *ratio decidendi* refers to the irreducible minimum of the reason why that outcome fits those facts. That reasoning is binding on the courts below, so we try to have a clear *ratio* in our cases. Lawyers and academics will sometimes complain that we don't, but we do try. And we usually have one Justice who is detailed to write the lead judgment. The other Justices can chip in with suggested amendments and improvements. We try to work collaboratively. Justices can add separate concurrences, but – we hope – not reaching the same conclusion for different reasons, because that would confuse everybody as to what the *ratio* is.

Justices can dissent. It's always possible, in the common law tradition, for people to disagree with the majority view. This is not the tradition in continental

Europe. In that tradition, dissent is an unusual and, in some cases, abhorrent idea, but we think it's not a bad thing. It's a good safety valve, and it also means that the decision of the majority does not have to compromise principle for the sake of bringing the minority on board. And sometimes today's dissent becomes tomorrow's majority view. I dissented in a case to do with something which is officially called the 'removal of the spare room subsidy', known colloquially as the 'bedroom tax'. I dissented in relation to one aspect of that case and the European Court of Human Rights in Strasbourg agreed with me, which was satisfying. But, of course, the greater the number of the judges who agree, the greater the authority of the decision. One would like to think that a unanimous decision of all eleven Justices of the Supreme Court, as the judgment against the prorogation of Parliament was, has an authority greater than it would have had if it had been a majority decision, especially if the majority had been a narrow one.

This process of judicial reasoning, is, or at least should be, the opposite of what the advocates do. Stephen Sedley, a retired Court of Appeal judge, writing extra-judicially before he became a full-time judge, said that what advocates do is 'reason from a given conclusion'. When you think about it, it's obvious: as an advocate, you listen to your client's story and problem, you work out what is the best result that the client could possibly hope for from the court, you advise your client that that is the best you can do, in order to manage their expectations, and then you work out how to persuade the court of that conclusion. So, advocates start at the end and work back to see how they can get the court to agree with their end, whereas judges should start at the beginning with the legal materials and the legal principles, and reason from them to the conclusion. I would like to suggest that we always do that, but I think that would be over-idealistic of me. I can't be too starry-eyed. We must always test the conclusion that we reach against our intuitive sense of justice and practicality.

There is also a certain amount of pragmatism built into legal principles, and this is a challenge. In two lectures I delivered in 2019 in Cambridge, on 'Principle and Pragmatism in Private Law' and on 'Principle and Pragmatism in Public Law', I found examples where an element of pragmatism was turned into a so-called principle by the law. For example, in private law, identifying a new duty of care in negligence is only done where this is fair, just, and reasonable. Now, that sounds like a principle but, basically, it is naked pragmatism. And so, also, in public law, there is a practice of deference – that is, respect for decisions made by public authorities. That too is dressed up as a principle but, actually, it's a largely pragmatic consideration as to who is best able to reach the decision in question, in the circumstances in question. So, we road-test the end result against a degree of principle and a degree of pragmatism, and the law itself has some concepts which themselves are redolent of pragmatism.

How does all this compare with how a painter goes about his work?

Hughie O'Donoghue

Artists make judgements, fine-tuning them to get somewhere specific in their art. And there's a moral dimension which is fundamental to our work.

Art's goal, towards which the fine-tuning of judgement is directed, is truth. The Victorian cultural commentator John Ruskin said that nations write their autobiographies in three books: the book of their words, the book of their deeds, and the book of their art. And although it's impossible to understand any one of the three books without reference to the other two, the only one you can trust to tell the truth is the book of art. We might think that words – the histories – tell us the truth, but they are partial. You only have to read, for instance, accounts of the Dunkirk evacuation from the perspectives of the French, the British, and the Germans for an example of how different the emphases of historians are. Artists have no axe to grind, so they come closer to the truth than historians, and they get there sooner.

By art, I don't mean history painting. When artists tried that, they too were not telling the truth. History painting was for many years regarded as the highest form of art, but it fell flat on its face and died about 150 years ago. It had become exhausted; it was predictable, theatrical, and propagandist. It was rejected by radical and ambitious artists. Think of a painting of Washington crossing the Delaware River, or of the coronation of Napoleon, or some heroic hussar on a horse somewhere. You know you are not being shown the truth.

In 1917, history painting was still commonplace. In the many contemporary histories of the 'Great War', as it was then known, most of the illustrations are in these redundant forms: heroised 'Tommies', demonised 'Huns'. No one would dream of portraying war in that way now, though some films still lapse into that idiom – even good ones such as *Saving Private Ryan* and *1917*.

But in 1917, in New York, Marcel Duchamp produced his famous urinal, *Fountain*. He was perhaps trying to show his disgust with the world, and possibly also with himself. The urinal is radical art expressing a loss of belief in the world order and in belief systems themselves: religions, monarchies, governments. The art movement with which Duchamp is associated is called Dada, a nonsense word a bit like 'goo-goo' or 'ga-ga'.

Duchamp's ironic urinal coincided with the irony of the Nivelle Offensive of 1917, and is an example of what I mean about the artist being closer to the truth than historians. In 1917, the common feeling was that civilisation was in the gutter. It was the bleakest of times. Even after the great slaughter of the Somme and Verdun, things were carrying on as before, but the common man had had enough. The soldiers walked forward in the Nivelle Offensive in a desultory manner, impersonating sheep en route to the abattoir. It was their expression of irony. That year, there were mutinies and insurrection in both the French and the British armies. Duchamp somehow captured that; he marked this moment in history when, as some have put it, deference died.

Also being produced in 1917 was a work of art – in fact, a series of works – that I think is even more radical than Duchamp's *Fountain*. It is Claude Monet's *Water Lilies*. Duchamp, who was thirty and hence of military age, fled France for the safety of New York, but Monet, at seventy-seven, remained in his studio in Giverny, a day's march from the front line. He said that he would rather die there than surrender to the German army. And he painted lilies. I think Monet was more radical, certainly braver, than Duchamp. Right up against the front line, his lilies showed an example of the triumph of culture over barbarism. Georges Clemenceau, the French president, believed as much. The very first trip he made out of Paris at the end of the war was to Monet's studio, because he wanted the paintings for the French nation.

I think artists often get closer to the truth than historians because they think differently. But it's often hard for artists to articulate what we're doing, because when we're doing it we actually don't really know what we're doing.

Brenda Hale

You have talked about truth, and about irony, and you've also talked about not knowing what you're doing when you're doing it. Of course, the process judges use, which I've described, is very conscious. If we don't know what we're doing, well, then we shouldn't be doing it, in my job. So, what do you think we judges can learn from you painters that would make us do our judging even better than we believe, or hope, that we do it now?

Hughie O'Donoghue

I think, in a way, the common ground that we have is an idea of the truth, an idea of fairness. We know that there's no such thing as a universal truth, but we do know what our own truth is. I think that judges learn from something that is evolving in the common mind. If we recall the soldiers at the Nivelle Offensive of 1917, I don't think the French army ever attacked after that. They had mutinies, and they never went forward again. But as I said, the penny dropped first with the artists. So, judges could learn from the artist that things aren't set in stone. Truth is a fugitive thing, and you have to pursue it. You can't say 'because this held true 100 years ago, it holds true now', and so you've got to be constantly alert. It's like language. You could argue that as soon as language is written down it becomes obsolete, because language changes. The vernacular is constantly evolving; spoken language responds fluidly to the needs of the time, much more so than written language. It means that neither artists nor judges can rest on their laurels, but artists can show soonest how our consciousness changes.

Brenda Hale
And the law is a moving thing, just as the truth is a moving thing. Justice is a moving thing. They are all developing.

Audience member
Lady Hale, you talked about principles and pragmatism, and you agreed with Hughie about the lack of universal truths, but how then would you define a principle of

legal justice? From where would you derive it? Because I would assume that there is something universal about a principle of legal justice.

Brenda Hale

There isn't a single legal principle. The principle will depend on what problem it is addressing. Speaking not from theory but from a practical judging point of view, there is an idea, for example, that if somebody is wrongfully harmed by another person, they should be properly compensated for that. The idea of justice is both that there should be compensation, and that the compensation should be a proper and fair reflection of the harm that's been done, the loss that has been suffered. Not a penny more, not a penny less. That is a concrete principle of justice, and there are many more like it, all hopefully reflecting an idea of justice: principles which treat people fairly, prevent harm to people, keep people to their promises. But an overarching principle of what the best justice is? I don't think that exists, because truth and justice are movable feasts. Take, for example, social justice, which underlies a lot of legal development now. It would not have been regarded as a principle of justice two centuries ago. That people should be treated equally, without regard to irrelevant qualities like their gender, or their ethnicity, or their religion, or their sexuality is a very new idea, a late-twentieth-century idea. I think it's the greatest development there has been in my professional lifetime, the notion that equality is, in fact, a principle of justice that we ought to do our best to respect. But it's new.

Audience member

Sometimes, technicality gets in the way of the truth in cases. I wondered how you felt about that.

Brenda Hale

Yes, it does. It particularly gets in the way of fact-finding. There's a truth in ideas, there's a truth in principles, and there's a truth in facts. A lot of legal proceedings are about trying to work out what on earth happened, who did what to whom, and this is really difficult to do. It's particularly difficult in cases where there aren't written materials which attest, contemporaneously, to what's been going on. If you only have oral evidence, you have problems about whom you believe.

We used to have a lot of very technical rules about what was permitted as evidence and what was not. We still have quite a lot of them in criminal cases, not just about what is evidence but also about what the jury can or can't be told. This is no longer the case in most family and civil cases, where the cases are person against person rather than state against person. Now, those rules in criminal cases are there to protect the accused. They're there to re-enforce the burden and standard of proof, which is that a person is presumed to be innocent until they're proven to be guilty, that the burden of proving their guilt lies with the prosecution, and that the prosecution has to prove guilt to the criminal standard, which is beyond reasonable doubt – or 'sure', which is what juries are now told they must be if they are to find the accused guilty. All of these technical rules get in the way of telling the jury everything that the jury might want to know.

There's another example where technicalities can get in the way. This is the advocate barrister's supreme ability to overcomplicate simple issues. The more money that is involved in a civil case, the more printing ink gets spilled in devising complexities in the hope that the judge will fall for one of those complexities. But that is the advocate's job, and it is the judge's task to detect what is going on and to see the wood for the trees.

So, you're quite right, sometimes technicality does get in the way. We judges do our best to overcome the second sort of technicality, but in the criminal courts the technical rules are there for a reason. Of course, if you sit on a jury and are sent out while there's an argument about whether somebody can say something to you, you'll be frustrated and you'll wonder what on earth the argument's about. If there's a lawyer on the jury, they can tell you, but they shouldn't. So, that's a problem too.

Audience member

Both of you spoke of envisioning justice as the pursuit of the truth. I wonder if, in both of your professions, you've perceived something to be true, but later, on reflection, you've perceived a different truth – and, if so, how you handled that.

Hughie O'Donoghue

Simply put, yes. The truth is a constantly shifting scenario for an artist, although a lot of artists recoil from that and retreat into style, or fashion, settling for one thing and keeping on doing that. In my view, the obligation of the artist is to do two things: work hard and tell the truth. The truth is the thing we can't grasp. We keep thinking we've got to some point of certainty about something, and then it moves on again. But keeping on trying to tell the truth is the artist's obligation. I think the greatest artist – not necessarily the greatest painter, but the greatest artist – is Vincent van Gogh. His attempts to be straightforward, to tell the truth, are painful. He's quite clumsy. He has all sorts of problems, but there's nothing as compelling as Van Gogh's drawings, or his letters, or his paintings, and people get it. He's probably the most popular artist in the world. I think that is something to do with the fact that he comes quite close to this truth. When I think of Van Gogh paintings, I think that this is a religious fanatic who's become disillusioned, and his paintings of the landscape are his paintings of God; they are his version of the truth. He's somebody constantly searching, and people, I think, understand that when they look at Van Gogh's paintings, without necessarily being able to articulate it.

Art's truth is subjective, and so all views about art are subjective. Michelangelo isn't a great artist because it says so in a book. Art is a particular kind of communication that involves things like faith and something felt, rather than something factual. And that throws the artist and the viewer back on their human emotions.

Brenda Hale

In my line of work, I have to believe that there are some things that are objectively true. The speed limit is 30 mph. If you exceed the speed limit, you will commit a criminal offence – not a very serious one, but you will. There is much in the law that is true in that mundane objective sense, but there are also areas of the law that are not wholly objectively true: they are matters of judgement and of dispute. The law is quite frequently contested.

That is what the Supreme Court is for. As an example,

a mundane one, we've been hearing a case for two days about where a dispute about a lot of money should be heard. Should it be heard in England, or should it be heard in another country? I went into the hearing thinking the answer to each of the issues was x, y, z, but I came out of the hearing, and our later discussion of the case, thinking the answer to those issues was a, b, and c. I'd perceived a different truth as a result of listening to the arguments, reading some of the materials, discussing it with my colleagues. I know that others of my colleagues went through exactly the same process, going into the hearing thinking one thing, and coming out of it thinking another.

Audience member

Would you say something about how you prevent your work being overly influenced by concerns about the immediate reaction to it?

Hughie O'Donoghue

Yes, one's work can be over-influenced by people's reactions. I think that is a profound problem of being an artist. The reason why I think Van Gogh is the greatest artist is that he was a compulsive truth-teller in his art. Not selling any of it while he was creating it was a great assistance to him in telling the truth. He sold almost none of his paintings, and although that is part of his tragic story it meant he didn't actually have to worry about the audience. Any artist who gets a bit of success is influenced by it, often in the most unexpected ways. When I had a bit of success, I found it very, very difficult. It brought me to a full stop with my work. I was really comfortable with my work when I didn't expect anybody to like it, but as soon as people started paying money for it, I started questioning my own integrity, and found it very, very problematic. And yet it is this precious thing of telling the truth that we want from our artists.

Brenda Hale

In this country and in most, if not all, modern Western liberal democracies, it is a cardinal principle that justice is done in the open, that we don't sit behind closed doors, that people can come and watch our hearings. In the Supreme Court, cases are live-streamed over the internet, so anybody can watch our hearings anywhere in the world, if they've got access to the internet. It's very important that we do our work in the open. Not only that, it's also important that we explain our decisions, as I described.

The principle of open justice has been there for a long time for two reasons: one is that we should explain to people in a coherent way what we've decided and why, and the other is that we are accountable to the public and to the higher courts, if there are any. So, open justice is both a discipline and an education. It means that, from time to time, our decisions are going to be criticised. We always hope that any criticism is expressed in moderate and sensible terms, and mostly it is. There are occasions when it is not so expressed. The most famous was when in 2016 the Lord Chief Justice, the Master of the Rolls, and a Lord Justice (Philip Sales, who later became a Justice of the Supreme Court), sitting in the Divisional Court of the High Court, were labelled 'enemies of the people' in a certain newspaper. Now, that sent a chill running down quite a few spines – and not only legal ones. Their decision, incidentally, was completely conventionally and constitutionally correct. But we have a free press which is entitled to say these things, as long as it stays within the realms of the law, and this accusation wasn't illegal.

That chilly criticism could have been answered by the Lord Chancellor, who has a statutory responsibility to uphold the rule of law and the independence of the judiciary. Her script would have been easy to write. It would have gone something like this:

In this country, we have a free press. We are very proud of our free press, and it's an important part of our constitution. However, it is my duty, as the member of government who is charged with defending the independence of the judiciary and the rule of law, to tell the newspaper in question that it was wrong. These were three very senior judges, who were doing their job, deciding a case in accordance with the law. If they had been wrong, they would have been put right by the Supreme Court, and they weren't.

That is an easy script, which could have been written immediately after the headline was published. Unfortunately, it didn't happen, but every subsequent Lord Chancellor has leapt to the judiciary's defence as needed and without hesitation.

The script could have gone on. It would have been riskier, but it could have said:

Beware what you wish for. If you are a newspaper that purports to uphold the rule of law and you treat the members of the judiciary who are doing their job like this, you are undermining the very thing you want to support.

Judges have to do our job according to the principles I have described, in the glare of publicity, in the knowledge that some of our decisions will not be popular. We swear an oath to do right to all manner of people after the laws and usages of this realm, without fear or favour, affection or ill will. I've sworn that oath five times now, and it still makes me want to cry.

Bureaucracy Should Be Beautiful: The Musician and the Permanent Secretary

Clare Moriarty and James O'Donnell
Written by Clare Moriarty

Introduction

Music, the Abbey, and public service were woven together throughout this event. The dialogue took place in the Lady Chapel of Westminster Abbey – home place of the Order of the Bath, which celebrates public service, both military and civilian. Our speaker was James O'Donnell, Organist and Master of the Choristers at the Abbey and a superb musician with a huge breadth of experience and a deep understanding of the Abbey's mission. As his bureaucrat interlocutor, I brought long immersion in the Civil Service and even longer roots as a choral singer. And many of the audience, as they told us when we opened up the dialogue to wider discussion, also had music in their veins as well as public service in their bones.

From the earliest stage of planning the dialogue, we

wanted it to embrace an experience of, as well as a discussion about, music. This element was provided by the Elysian Singers choir, which represents for me a personal meeting point between bureaucracy and music. I was involved in setting up the choir in my very early days in the Civil Service, while in recent years I've found Monday evening rehearsals a welcome antidote to the challenges of Public Accounts Committee hearings, change programmes, and complex policy. The Lady Chapel provided a wonderful setting in which to hear this excellent choir performing, under the direction of Sam Laughton, four pieces matched to the themes of the dialogue.

The first half of the dialogue was a conversation between James and me, punctuated by musical contributions from the Elysian Singers; in the second half, we broadened the discussion to the audience. Under the heading – or provocation – of 'bureaucracy should be beautiful', the dialogue ranged widely in pursuit of understanding about how the public good is served through both music and the Civil Service. We examined the parallels between making music and making policy, explored leadership in our respective domains, and converged on the centrality to both of authentic being.

Incurably bureaucratic, I started with some framing to give structure and shape to the dialogue. Reflecting on leadership roles that I've held, I identified three things they had in common. All of them, broadly speaking, were about getting stuff done; all involved making things happen through people; and all involved connecting with the world outside, where the impact of the Civil Service's work is felt. I could see parallels for each of these in music: parallels for getting things done, in composing music; for making it happen through people, in turning the musical notation into performance; and for connecting with the world outside, in the effect that music has on the audience.

I didn't know in advance how well this trio of parallels would stand up – whether they would resonate with James, or feel like an artificial construct. They proved a useful way of structuring our conversation and found a mirror in something that James described as a 'triangle of interpretation', linking the composer creating a piece, performers interpreting it, and the listener receiving it. Our two triangles in turn broadly correspond to three of the four themes that emerged from the dialogue and discussion: creativity in getting stuff done, composing in particular; leadership to create performance through people; and connection with the audience listening and responding to the music. The fourth theme, development, can be seen as occupying the centre of the triangle, bringing all of the elements together in an appreciation of what it takes to be a musician or civil servant.

Creativity

The theme of creativity emerged early in the dialogue, as James and I began talking about getting stuff done. My Civil Service analogy was that, in developing a new policy, we start with the overall direction that ministers have decided to take and then break it down into chunks. We work through a lot of detail, often involving complex negotiation within and between government departments, before some kind of product emerges, perhaps in the form of a White Paper or consultation document.

When I put this process to James, he recognised it in musical terms as writing to a commission, and he immediately viewed it through the lens of its impact on creativity. For a composer, a commission that sets the direction for a piece of music, and even fixes some parameters, isn't necessarily a brake on creativity but rather a shaping of it. Far from railing against the constraints of a commission, they will embrace the narrowing of a potentially infinite range of options as a stimulus for their creative work, seeking a steer from the commissioner of the piece to understand what they really want from it.

Creativity goes deep in composition. James talked about the idea that, rather than building the music out of notes, the composer catches and brings into realisation something that is already there. That felt immediately appealing to me, but isn't an obvious fit with how a civil servant might talk about policymaking. It's not that creativity is an alien concept to civil servants, or that there is no place for it in policy, but we tend to see 'big sweep' creativity as the preserve of politicians, while civil servants focus on the practical space of implementation. The distinction between creativity of the 'what' and of the 'how' does, though, seem to be a space of parallels between music and policymaking.

James described a complex environment where there are, in theory, huge degrees of freedom in how an artist gets from a concept to the finished article but also, in practice, all sorts of conventions to navigate. Historically, you see examples of that in the visual arts, with French academic painters having developed highly prescriptive approaches and imposed them widely on pain of exclusion from the scheme of consideration.

In music, this question of a 'right way' of doing things surfaces in the debate about historically informed performance. In the last few decades, there has been a school of thinking that music should be performed as it would have been heard when first composed. In the early stages of this movement, the attachment to historical accuracy was taken to great lengths. Original texts were regarded as inviolable – authoritative almost to the point of being fetishised – along with contemporary treatises on how instruments should be played. The resulting faithful reproduction of earlier performances came at the expense of the musician's own individuality of expression. It was almost as if 'permission to perform' depended on subordinating individual interpretation to the historically accurate approach.

If this feels to a civil servant like extreme prescription, we should remember that similar strictures applied in our world too. Not that long ago, Civil Service communications were highly prescribed, down to the precise layout of a submission and style of address for colleagues as well as external correspondents. James said that he can identify a German choir by the sound they make, reflecting a particular style of singing. I suspect it would have been similarly easy to identify a civil servant's department by examining a memo or minute they had written.

In both music and the Civil Service, there is a sense that rigid rules have relaxed in recent years. James described the current composing environment as a very eclectic world where the 'stuff' of 'getting stuff done' is almost anything that a composer wants it to be, and similarly much of the formality of Civil Service working has dissipated.

However, the debate about prescription versus flexibility – and space for creativity – has not gone away, but rather changed and adapted. In the question and answer session, one person recalled, from her musical education, being taught to sing and play the violin in a certain way. She drew a parallel with finding a strong attachment in the Civil Service to particular ways of doing things, to the point where achieving high standards of process feels more important than outcomes. How, she asked, could we maintain focus on the problems we're trying to solve, the lives we want to improve, the changes we want to make?

This seems to me a deeply important question for the Civil Service. As public servants, we are held to account and have to be able to justify the decisions that we make. It's an important part of our professional identity to maintain high standards of rigour – to do things the right way. That means that there are areas where attachment to process is objectively important. However, there are plenty of others where it feels more like habit and a preference for conformity, and as such it is crying out for someone to come along and challenge received wisdom. By clipping our wings when we don't need to, we miss opportunities for creativity, and the resulting output is never as good as it could be.

There is an obvious parallel with musical composition, and indeed performance. While musicians are not held to account in the way that civil servants are, the pressure to conform, to uphold musical purity, clearly exists for them too. Just as in the Civil Service, there is a balance to be struck between honouring and challenging accepted ways of doing things. In music, that means respecting the underlying purpose of the musical 'rules' while leaving space for individual interpretation and creative boundary-pushing.

Stylistic continuity tends to keep performance in gradual evolution rather than sudden revolution. It is evident that in music, as in policymaking, there can be no major advances if everyone stays within a prescribed style. That evolution may become more refined over time, but by definition it does not permit radical change. In policymaking, the conditions for radical change are often created by newly elected governments bringing different ideologies, perspectives, and priorities to the business of government. Music has no equivalent of general elections to drive change, so any step change in style must come from some transgression of the rules.

James gave some examples of moments when the musical world has been presented with extremely new approaches, statements of individual vision about how music should sound that could be quite shocking to others. When singers specialising in early music adopted an approach of singing without any vibrato, it felt almost provocative, making the point that this was different music being given a different type of performance. The unfamiliarity of the sound underlined the fact that it came not from an evolved, developed accrual of performance, practices, and traditions but was deliberately rethought and reinvented on the basis of historical research and personal creative imagination.

Leadership

Exploring the role of the conductor provided insights into the parallels between musical and Civil Service leadership. In a Civil Service context, making things happen through people is the core of leadership, and I was interested to hear how leading a team compares with the experience of conducting, creating an ensemble performance from a group of players or singers.

In conducting, as in team leadership, there is no 'one size fits all' approach. A performance with a 'scratch' choir or orchestra, which creates a burst of energy as people come together on an ad hoc basis and gel quickly, has a very different context from Westminster Abbey, or an orchestra with a long-standing conductor – the Hallé Orchestra with Mark Elder, or the City of Birmingham Symphony Orchestra with Simon Rattle, for example. Whatever the scenario, the same question arises: how does the conductor add value? With a scratch ensemble, the conductor has a decisive role requiring full and visible presence, capturing a working operational dynamic in the room with everyone's antennae on full twitch. In an environment of long-term relationships, the conductor is working much more gradually to deepen and build practice, day on day.

Leadership, though, is measured by its impact on those who are led. James shared an anecdote of a musician arriving late for an engagement after a rehearsal where he'd been leading the orchestra. Asked who was conducting, he replied, 'I don't know; I never looked'. While possibly apocryphal, this story made its point clearly: members of an ensemble may not be at all convinced that the conductor is adding value. In a professional orchestra, every member is a highly competent practitioner who, left to their own devices, will play the music as they think it should go, or the way they're used to playing. Very few conductors can play more than one or two instruments, at most, to the level of proficiency required of their orchestra members, so the conductor's role is not mainly one of giving technical guidance or asking for a particular style of playing.

This had very direct parallels for me with my experience as Director General for Rail at the Department for Transport, where I found myself in charge of a team of rail experts and commercial specialists whose technical expertise I could comprehend but not hope to match. That presented a considerable challenge in adding value to their work, and required a very deliberate response when I had to arbitrate between the strongly held views of different specialist groups. I found the solution partly in consciously creating the conditions for mutual respect – mine for the expertise of the specialists, theirs for my ability to navigate the political landscape – and partly in listening very carefully and trusting my instincts to reveal the right path.

Listening to James talk about his own experience of conducting, I felt that he was describing something very similar. The way that a conductor adds value doesn't come from following a prescribed process. Indeed, James said that it depended on not consciously thinking about what he was doing. Interpreting a piece of music is a matter less of translating precise musical notation into sound, and more of using the notation as a starting point for working out where the music is. James said that when he found himself self-consciously thinking, 'Am I doing this too fast? Am I being clear enough? What am I doing here?' the result was a stilted performance, as the sense of the music was lost. The music flowed when he thought about its overall trajectory and his role in directing it there, letting people be part of it.

James described conducting as giving a sense of context, moulding a constantly changing organic process, creating a sense of everybody coming together and fitting the performance into a shape. There is an important element of conducting technique, and the skill and craft of conducting can be taught and learnt. But James underlined the subtle nature of a conductor's communication, using non-verbal and 'personality' signals more than words. Some very eminent and wonderful conductors have hardly said anything in rehearsal and have scarcely 'conducted' in a visible sense, yet they have created astonishing performances.

This aligns perfectly with my sense of leadership at its best as an almost unconscious process that relies on seeing and projecting the whole beyond the component parts. For both conductor and Civil Service leader, drilling forensically into the detail is sometimes required, but this constantly needs to be balanced with a sense of holding the whole, which falls apart if you look too hard at any one component.

James referred to this as 'intuition', describing the musician's lifelong project of informing their intuition in order to connect directly and deeply with music, so that their focus is on the musical 'being' as a whole, rather than on the 'doing' of the component parts. Intuition is less commonly talked about in the Civil Service, often seen as antithetical to an approach strongly grounded in logic and reasoning. However, this both misunderstands intuition and overstates the degree of rationality in the best Civil Service approaches. I prefer to see intuition as a way of reaching logical conclusions more quickly than can be achieved through forward reasoning.

As a Civil Service leader, I found that two of my most powerful tools were ones I stumbled on inside myself and would now regard as uses of intuition. The first, which I discovered early in my career, was a 'logic detector' that I applied to structured argument. Reading a submission, I could 'feel' when there was a flaw in the argument, even if it took more time to locate where the flaw was. The other I called my 'dissonance meter', and it worked the same way but applied to people rather than argument. When what people said didn't seem to match up with the other signals they were giving, I used it as a way in to start conversations about what was actually going on.

Intuition and authenticity both came up in the question and answer session. One audience member recalled the sublime feeling of playing in an orchestra where the conductor's communication was largely unspoken. She contrasted that with the Civil Service tendency to spend a long time choosing the right words and drafting elegant sentences, and asked whether there was a parallel in the 'saying versus being' of authentic leadership.

That raised interesting questions for me. You can choose to equate the civil servant's carefully chosen words either with the composer's notes – the substance of the music – or with the conductor's direction to the musicians performing the music. The first analogy might apply to the words in a policy document; in leadership terms, the second analogy is closer. Either way, the choice of words (or notes) is hugely important, as they convey purpose and tone. As a Permanent Secretary, the place where I felt my own voice was most critical was in our internal communications. I allowed nothing to go out in my name unless I was personally happy with it and with how I felt it would land with the people in the department. That made for a fair amount of drafting time, which was a decision I made about how to prioritise my time. Equally, and to the questioner's point, it was very clear that words only mattered to the extent that they matched up with deeds and were received as heartfelt – in effect, as authentic. Like the questioner, I have found that my most profound experience of singing has been when the conductor doesn't need to communicate in words, but the singers just know what is being asked of them. That unspoken communication relies a lot on visual clues and I fear isn't fully translatable – or scalable – to leadership of an organisation where it is impossible, or rarely possible, for everyone to be in the same space together. But the closer we can get to it the better, and there is certainly an equivalence for Civil Service leaders in focusing on the atmosphere they create, trying to make it possible for everyone to give their best, rather than giving specific instruction in words.

Connection

Our dialogue continued into the space where performance and performers meet the audience. In exploring this dimension, my starting point was a personal belief that most public policy only becomes real when it connects with people. Policy created in the abstract – however well informed by philosophy, experience, and international comparisons – is inevitably bounded by prior expectations. It is lifeless until it comes into contact with those who are affected by it or invested in it, and it is suboptimal unless their experience in turn feeds into and informs it. This is part of how policy connects with the audience and is also shaped by it.

In the context of music, that raises a philosophical question of what is needed for music to be complete. Can a composition fully be considered a piece of music if it's never performed? And would it matter if its performance only ever took place in a closed room, without an audience? James was clear that a piece of music can exist in the abstract without being performed to an audience or indeed without ever being played. It's still a piece of music, with intrinsic value – but it has unrealised dimensions until the triangle of interpretation is complete: the composer composing a piece, performers performing it, and the listener receiving it. In particular, without the opportunity to communicate the music beyond those directly involved in creating it, something is missing. The term James used, of music being 'actuated' through performance, conveys the same sense as policy coming to life through connection with the world outside.

In the dynamic of a musical performance, the process of listening is active, not passive, and performers draw energy from the audience. Performing a piece of organ music in a packed, expectant, and resonant cathedral feels quite different to performing the same piece to a thin audience in a venue with a flat acoustic. Any performer will have in mind how the music they're playing lands with the audience. At the same time, with as many ways of listening to a particular piece as there are listeners, James felt that it was fruitless to second-guess how an audience would receive a performance: the performer's goal must be to develop their own interpretation of the music and execute it to the very best of their ability.

In policymaking, the same doesn't hold good. Public policy is bounded by what is politically acceptable, and is often communicated in the way judged to have the highest likelihood of making an impact or securing desired behaviour change. Choosing the right message is part of good policymaking, which is also in a constant dynamic relationship with the experience of those affected by it. Policy that ploughs on regardless of what comes up through feedback loops is rarely sustainable. That is in contrast with music, where tailoring a performance to suit the audience – an obvious temptation in competitive situations where the preferences of jury members may be well known – risks losing the performer's authentic voice.

As with many other aspects, though, the difference is one of degree rather than absolute. Being sensitive to the audience is intrinsic to the nature of policy in a democratic society, and doesn't challenge its integrity in the way that tailoring a performance to the tastes of the audience might be felt by a musician to do. However, that is not the same as being entirely audience-driven.

Many of the difficult judgements made in government concern the meeting point between technocracy and democracy, which can feel like competing versions of good. Making those judgements with care and sensitivity doesn't feel too far from developing an interpretation and executing it to the best of one's ability. And, conversely, the musician's challenge of remaining true to underlying principles and also responsive to the audience is familiar to civil servants charged with remaining impartial and objective while serving democratically elected governments.

Development

Development was the least obvious theme to emerge from our dialogue. It was neither present in my 'starter for ten' framework nor immediately visible in James's triangle of interpretation. Yet the fact that so many roads in our dialogue led back to personal and professional development is perhaps a sign of how important it is to both musicians and civil servants.

I was interested to understand the relationship between practice and performance for a musician. There is no direct analogy for the Civil Service. Policymaking consists of a lot of detailed work culminating in major moments, for example when a document is published. I started off with the idea that the detailed work was the 'practice' to the publication's 'performance'. However, the performative element – a statement to the House of Commons, or a media round – is generally political, while virtually all of the civil servant's work takes place behind the scenes. Arguably, the Civil Service is all practice and no performance, reflected in the term 'practitioner' to the musician's 'performer'.

Even in the musical world, though, with terminology dominated by performance and effort directed towards it, day-to-day reality is much more about practice. Most musicians spend the vast majority of their time playing on their own. A concert pianist will spend 95 per cent of their life practising alone and 5 per cent in front of an audience. So, the value and purpose of practice are centrally important. The hours of solo practice put in by a concert pianist, or an organist, contribute towards the quality of their eventual performance. The performance itself, however, may only attract a small audience, perhaps because the music has a niche following. Does that matter, or is the act of practising – to become better at what you're playing – sufficient in itself?

James recognised the disappointment that is felt by a musician when months of preparation culminate in performing to a handful of people, without the energy generated by a bigger audience. However, for a musician, practising is part of who you are, like breathing, or getting up in the morning, or having a shower. Playing music alone is also a source of satisfaction as well as an important way of discovering yourself as a musician.

There is a paradox in that the necessity of practice is poorly recognised in the prevailing economic model for professional musicians. Very few have the luxury of stable musical employment in a cathedral or orchestra; most are paid on the basis of performances given. Arguably that doesn't matter, provided performance fees are set at a level which covers the cost of personal practice, rehearsal, and expenses. However, the signalling is important, and in some cases the impact becomes very stark. An opera singer who takes on a big role in a distant city and has to withdraw from a performance at the last minute due to illness will find themself significantly out of pocket.

This is a degree of precarity, even at the highest levels, which is unfamiliar to civil servants who are paid for continuous service. It was brought into stark relief by the onset of the coronavirus pandemic. With performances taken off the agenda, many musicians saw their livelihoods entirely removed. Their personal practice no doubt did continue, but their income disappeared. Civil servants, meanwhile, continued working through the pandemic, with stable employment but carrying the huge load of responding to the needs of the country while having to find new ways of working.

The narrative of development is found in both music and the Civil Service, though it plays out differently in the two worlds. As a career civil servant, I developed predominantly by progressing through different roles, moving from advising to leading as I became more senior and my responsibilities broadened. I acquired skills along the way largely by doing, initially under supervision and then independently as I became more experienced. There was plenty that I couldn't do technically in my early years and learned how to do later.

If the civil servant's development trajectory is substantially about broadening, the musician's might be characterised as equally about deepening. James gave the example of someone conducting Beethoven's *Fifth Symphony* as a twenty-year-old at university with a college orchestra, and then returning to it ten years later with a different orchestra. The intervening ten years of performance, study, and musical development mean that while both performances may be good, they will be different – a product of the conductor's maturity and the context as well as each orchestra's technical prowess.

This distinction was picked up by an audience member who asked what it takes for someone to be 'orchestra-ready' as a public servant, noting that an inexperienced violin player wouldn't be considered ready to join an orchestra whereas a new recruit to the Civil Service was immediately regarded as able to take on a role. An obvious answer to this, reflecting the development paths of both civil servants and musicians, is that the challenge is to find the right level of orchestra for one's skills at the time. Aged eight with a squeaky violin, I was (just) ready for my primary school orchestra, but I wasn't about to rock the Royal Albert Hall any more than I could have drafted a submission. The right orchestra for any of us changes over time, and we should keep refining the skills that allow us to play in the best possible orchestra for the level of skill that we're able to develop.

However, the question also shone a light on the

difference between amateurs and professionals. It's possible to be a professional civil servant and an amateur musician, and plenty of people who were present at the dialogue met that description. But the converse doesn't hold: there's no such thing as an amateur civil servant. That's perhaps too obvious to be worth remarking upon, but it flows through to the way that different skills are learned. Most people gain musical skills around the edges of an educational process that equips us much more directly with the capability we need to be civil servants: not just the three Rs but basic analysis, synthesis, and reasoning skills.

The experience of training to become a professional musician is quite different. For some, including the Westminster Abbey choristers, it starts early. The training they receive is not just in choral and vocal technique but more broadly aimed at developing them to be good musicians in an ensemble: sensitive to their surroundings, able to breathe together and predict what each other will do. James likened singing in the choir to playing on a football team or operating in a very complicated social environment. The aim is to develop musical skill alongside the growth of musicality in a more holistic sense.

For any professional musician, development is a lifelong pursuit. When James said that the only person a musician ultimately has to satisfy in their music-making is themself, it didn't sound like a soft option. He explained that the point of spending your life studying music, deepening competence and knowledge, is to improve your self-awareness as a musician. He referred to the delight of constantly developing musical understanding through discovery: coming across someone bringing a new interpretation to a piece that you know well, or hearing it differently because of other music you've come across since you last played or heard it. That sense of constantly seeing familiar things in a new light drives the musician's interpretation and approach, and ultimately keeps them at the task of constantly seeking to improve their performance.

Conclusion

Towards the end of our dialogue, as we drew the threads together, James said something that summed up the way music shapes his life. He talked about the sense of being on a circle, constantly working out where he is on it and finding it was bigger than he had thought. He described the life of a musician as about not just making music – whether by composing or performing – but something more profound, about 'being' rather than 'doing'. For a musician, there is an imperative to make music. James said that he had, on various occasions, asked himself whether professional music was the right course for him, but each time he had come to the inescapable conclusion that he really couldn't do anything else. This alignment came over, and he named it, as a vocational element to being a musician: a really deep connection with music.

James's point about music as 'being, not doing' went to the heart of the original 'exam question': would greater dialogue with the arts help policymakers? The deep connection that people experience with music goes beyond the sound it makes to more fundamental truths. This mirrors the deep connection to the impacts of policies developed and implemented by civil servants on the lives of citizens and communities. It feels obvious that greater understanding between the two disciplines can only lead to better policy.

Two contributions in the post-dialogue discussion served to illustrate this. One member of the audience talked about how music creates delight and wonder for her, and asked whether it could feature more in our thinking about policy. Another drew the connection to beauty and the scope for beauty embedded in the paraphernalia of bureaucracy – from websites to buildings – to influence our experience of it positively. Both these points reflect the fundamental public service mission of making the world a better place. That must involve elements of delight, but it more frequently feels like a series of problems to be solved and things to be fixed. I was left feeling that if we could bottle the creativity and connection in music – its beauty, indeed – and bring them into policymaking as sources of delight and wonder, we could only improve our public service.

As we talked about intuition and authenticity alongside practice and performance, this strong sense of 'being, not doing' emerged as something for us to strive for in the world of policymaking and the Civil Service, embodying a deeper connection with people and their needs. For me personally, having spent the latter part of my Civil Service career advocating a more people-centred approach, it felt like a very natural conclusion. I would happily subscribe to the idea of a life's work of informing my intuition, and in turn allowing my intuition to guide my leadership. In the Civil Service, as in music, that must be a recipe for the best possible outcomes.

Choral contributions
From the Elysian Singers, directed by Sam Laughton

Judith Weir – 'Love Bade Me Welcome'
Here, Weir 'gets stuff done' by writing very precisely to her brief: taking a famous poem already full of religious allegory and adding just enough music to bring it further to life without overburdening it.

Antonio Lotti – 'Crucifixus à 8'

This is a classic example of 'building a team' in sound by gradually adding each of the eight parts in turn, each one adding a slightly different perspective to the existing sound.

Eric Whitacre – 'Lux Aurumque'

Whitacre has made a career from 'connecting with the audience', both by creating an immediate and attention-grabbing sound world and by his use of the internet and his profile to draw singers and listeners together.

Hubert Parry – 'My Soul, There is a Country'

Parry was passionate about his role in composing public and 'ethical' music, and in nurturing the next generation through his leadership of the Royal College of Music and his extraordinarily generous personality.

WESTMINSTER ABBEY INSTITUTE

Art, Imagination and Public Service is published in partnership with Westminster Abbey Institute. The Institute was founded by Westminster Abbey in 2013 to work with the people and institutions by whom it is surrounded in Parliament Square, to revitalise moral and spiritual values and virtues in public life. It offers space and time for challenging lectures, conversations, ideas, and quiet reflection.

In doing so, the Institute aims to remind those who govern of their vocation to public service, helping them to grow in moral sensitivity and resilience and to better define the good they are trying to do.

The material in this book does not necessarily represent the views of Westminster Abbey or its Institute.

HAUS CURIOSITIES

PUBLISHED WITH WESTMINSTER ABBEY INSTITUTE

The Power of Politicians
TESSA JOWELL AND FRANCES D'SOUZA

The Power of Civil Servants
DAVID NORMINGTON AND PETER HENNESSY

The Power of Judges
DAVID NEUBERGER AND PETER RIDDELL

The Power of Journalists
NICK ROBINSON, GARY GIBBON, BARBARA SPEED AND
CHARLIE BECKETT

The Responsibilities of Democracy
JOHN MAJOR AND NICK CLEGG

Integrity in Public Life
VERNON WHITE, CLAIRE FOSTER-GILBERT AND
JANE SINCLAIR

Truth in Public Life
VERNON WHITE, STEPHEN LAMPORT AND
CLAIRE FOSTER-GILBERT

Secret Service
JONATHAN EVANS

Justice in Public Life
CLAIRE FOSTER-GILBERT, JAMES HAWKEY AND
JANE SINCLAIR

HAUS CURIOSITIES

Inspired by the topical pamphlets of the interwar years, as well as by Einstein's advice to 'never lose a holy curiosity', the series presents short works of opinion and analysis by notable figures. Under the guidance of the series editor, Peter Hennessy, Haus Curiosities have been published since 2014.

Welcoming contributions from a diverse pool of authors, the series aims to reinstate the concise and incisive booklet as a powerful strand of politico-literary life, amplifying the voices of those who have something urgent to say about a topical theme.

Citizens of Everywhere: Searching for Identity in the Age of Brexit
PETER GUMBEL

The London Problem: What Britain Gets Wrong About its Capital City
JACK BROWN

Unwritten Rule: How to Fix the British Constitution
STEPHEN GREEN, THOMAS LEGG AND MARTIN DONNELLY